SELECTED POEMS
OF
C.P. CAVAFY

First published in 1998
Reprinted in 2012
The Dedalus Press
13 Moyclare Road
Baldoyle
Dublin 13
Ireland

www.dedaluspress.com

ISBN 978 1 901233 26 1

Dedalus Press titles are represented in the UK by
Central Books, 99 Wallis Road, London E9 5LN
and in North America by Syracuse University Press, Inc.,
621 Skytop Road, Suite 110, Syracuse, New York 13244.

Cover image: Detail of *The Great Library of Alexandria*
by O. Von Corven, 19th century

The Dedalus Press receives financial assistance from
The Arts Council / An Chomhairle Ealaíon

SELECTED POEMS
OF
C.P. CAVAFY

Translated by
Desmond O'Grady

DEDALUS PRESS
DUBLIN, IRELAND

ACKNOWLEDGEMENTS:

The poems given here are versions from Cavafy's final, published texts. However, to give some idea of Cavafy's development I have arranged this selection in the chronological order in which they were first written according to that given in *C.P. Cavafy: Collected Poems,* translated by Edmund Keeley and Philip Sherrard, edited by George Savidis (Princeton University Press, 1975, 1980), and in *Cavafy's Alexandria, A Study of a Myth in Progress* by Edmund Keeley (Harvard University Press, 1976). In realising my versions I have referred, for verisimilitude, to various other published versions, *The Poems of C.P. Cavafy* by John Mavrogordato (Hogarth Press, London 1951); *The Complete Poems of Cavafy* by Rae Dalven (New York 1961); and some translations into Italian and French.

A different version of 'Ionian' appeared as 'My Country' in *His Skaldcrane's Nest,* poems, Desmond O'Grady (Gallery Press 1970). Slightly different versions of 'One of Their Gods', under the title 'One of Them', and 'Expecting the Barbarians', under the title 'Waiting for the Barbarians', appeared in *The Writers: A Sense of Ireland,* ed. Andrew Carpenter and Peter Fallon (O'Brien Press, Dublin 1980). 'Cavafy in Alexandria' first appeared in *Alexandrian Notebook* (Raven Arts Press, Dublin 1989). For their Cavafy Symposium the Hellenic Foundation printed an early version of these translations as *Alternative Manners* (Alexandria 1993).

I am grateful to Dr. Doris Enright-Clark Shoukri and Dr. Nur Elmessiri of the English Department, The American University in Cairo for their hospitality while I was in Egypt and to the poet Kostis Moskof for inviting me back to Alexandria. I thank the Cultural Relations Committee of the Irish Department of Foreign Affairs for assistance in enabling me to complete this collection.

CONTENTS

⤨

Preface / 7

⤨

PREFACE

Born in Alexandria in Egypt in 1863, Constantine Peter Cavafy was the ninth and last child of well-off Greek parents from Constantinople, merchant families on both sides. The family moved temporarily to England in 1872, when Cavafy was nine, and remained there until he was sixteen when they returned permanently to Alexandria. While in England Cavafy became acquainted with the works of Shakespeare, Browning and Oscar Wilde. He became so at home with English manners and the language that he dressed in the English style and spoke Greek with a touch of an English accent until the day he died. His first verses were written in English, French and Greek during 1882 when he lived with his formidable mother Haricleia in Constantinople where and when, it seems, he had his first homosexual experiences.

Back in Alexandria in 1885 Cavafy worked as a part-time journalist and with his brother on the Egyptian Stock Exchange. He continued to write poems and some prose essays. At twenty-nine he got a clerical position in the Irrigation Service (Third Circle) of the Ministry of Public Works where he stayed for the next thirty years until 1922. He remained a Greek citizen living in Alexandria with his mother who died in 1899 and after that living alone until his own death from cancer of the larynx in 1933.

"It is recorded that he received the communion of the Orthodox Church shortly before he died and that his last motion was to draw a circle on a blank sheet of paper and then place a dot or full stop in the centre of the circle. As far as is known Cavafy had only one intimate long-standing relationship, with Alexander Singopoulos whom he designated his heir and literary executor some ten years before his death". (Keeley) His literary relationships included a twenty year acquaintance with E.M. Forster who introduced his work to T.E. Lawrence, Arnold Toynbee and T.S. Eliot who published 'Ithaka' in the *Criterion*.

Cavafy never offered a collection of his poems for sale during his lifetime. Instead he gave privately printed pamphlets and broadsheets to his close friends. His sophisticated modernity is all the more astonishing because it appeared so early, before most European 'moderns' and seemingly from nowhere, as though by instinct. He showed the way for the Greek poets who came after him towards solving the problem of modernising formal Greek with demotic language for writing contemporary poetry.

Generally Cavafy's importance as a poet went unnoticed in Greece and Europe until after his death. Now, through translation, he has been recognised as a major figure in modern European poetry. He found his mythic manner as early as 1894 in 'Ithaka', mastered it by 1898 in 'Expecting the Barbarians'. Long before his contemporaries, in the 1890s he saw the possibilities for a poetry of the mytho-historic imagination, a four-dimensional or cubist poetry, all on his own out on the fringe of Europe.

SELECTED POEMS OF
C.P. CAVAFY

Cavafy in Alexandria

He's hidden everywhere here;
not as he looks in his photographs
but in his psyche, habits:
his stylized diffidence,
conservative decadence. I glimpse,
detect him frequently: at night
walking quickly down an alley
close to the wall's shadow;
afternoon in a tea-room alone,
glancing over the edge of his
foreign newspaper, his eyeglasses;
mornings at his desk in the crowded
clerical bureaucracy where I must go
to regularise my papers.
He shows up behind one face
or another in any of his private poems;
they are in his glances. I may,
one afternoon or evening, be introduced,
perhaps approached by him for staring;
he sitting on the end edge
of a canapé, stiff in his correct,
if shabby suit and tie, turned-in toes;
peering from spectacles out of his
other-world expectancy. I feel
nervous about what to say then,
what talk about. Yes?

Desmond O'Grady

Candles

Our future days line forward
like a row of candles :
alight, golden, warm.

Our past days quench behind,
a gutted queue of burnt-out candles.
Those closest still smoke;
melted, cold, distorted.

I don't want to look back; seeing them I'd tremble.
How quickly the snuffed line lengthens.
How quickly burnt-out candles multiply.

August 1893

Footsteps

On his ebony bed, decorated
with coral eagles, lies Nero
asleep — happy, peaceful, callous,
at the height of his health,
in the vigour of his youth.

However, in the alabaster hallway
that houses his shrine of the Aenobarbi,
the household deities shift restlessly.
Those little gods shiver, fitfully
try to hide their innocuous bodies.
They've heard some sinister sound:
a deathly shuffle ascending the stairs,
a heavy plod plod on the staircase.
Then, flushed out by fear, these miserable
lares scamper and scuttle behind the shrine
shoving, stumbling over each other
because they know that sinister sound,
recognise the footsteps of the Furies.

August 1893

Ithaka

When you start your journey to Ithaka
make sure it's a long road, full
of adventures, new experiences. Make it your own
curiosity-collection of gathered knowledge, knowhow.
Have no fear of cannibal bogeymen
met in halflight, or those with one eye open
for their main chance, and face the dramatics
of Poseidon's theatrical seas fearlessly.
You need never truck with such threatening
mediocrity in your voyaging if your vision
stays steady on your horizon,
if your mind maintains its magnanimity.
You need never traffic with these cannibal
bogeymen, with those one-eyed chancers,
or suffer the tantrums of temperamental
seas if you don't ship such confusions
with you in the hold of your soul.
You need never have to deal
with these distractions unless
your soul trumps them up,
before your dazzled eyes.

Make sure your journey's a long one,
that your summers' dawns break
for many years. Sail into ports
you've never dreamed of, not seen before,
with a secure satisfaction, in silent certitude.
Meander through every marketplace you find.
Collect what materials you may need:
the prismatic amber of curiosity, the mother-
of-pearl that's fantasy and those pleasures that
please your senses. Acquire all that's available.
Stop in every city to meet, converse with anyone
of culture; cultivate curiosity of the imagination.

Keep Ithaka marked on your mind's map,
always. Arrival there is your final goal.
Don't hurry your journey in any way. Better
to last it for decades. As you age, anchor
at small islands with the wealth you've acquired
voyaging. Never expect Ithaka to give you anything.
Ithaka gave you the journey. Without her
you'd never have begun in the first place.
She has nothing else to give you.

If you find her wanting, Ithaka
has not cheated you. From the wisdom
you've gained, the knowledge you've absorbed,
the experience you've embodied
you'll understand by then
what these Ithakas mean.

January? 1894

Voices

Loved voices, idealized voices
of those dead, or of those
gone from us like the dead.

Occasionally they visit us in dreams.
Sometimes, thoughtful, we hear them.

Their voices echo the first poetry
of our lives for a moment,
like far off music fading at night.

12 July 1894

This City

You said, "I'll go to a different country, cross the sea,
find another, better city than this one.
Here everything I do goes wrong
and my heart is dead and buried as a corpse.
How long should my soul suffer here?
Wherever I turn, anywhere I look
I see the burnt cinders of my life here
where I've spent too long doing nothing."

You'll find no new sea, no new country.
This city will always dog you.
You'll roam the same streets,
go grey in the same houses.
You'll always end up here.
Forget anywhere else.
You've no ship, no road.
The life you've wasted here
you've wasted everywhere.

August 1894

Ionian

Although we've smashed their statues,
have thrown them out of their temples
the gods are not therefore dead,
Ionia, they still love you,
their very souls still remember.
When an August dawn awakens you
their presence permeates the air.
On occasion an ethereal youth —
vague, vigorous — soars over your hills.

October 1896

Windows

In these dark rooms to kill time
I mope about, look for windows.
When a window opens I'll feel release.
But I can't find a window —
or there are none. Better, perhaps.
The light may bring new terrors.
Who knows what it would reveal?

August 1897

Expecting the Barbarians

Why are we all waiting here in the square?

    The barbarians arrive today.

Why's nothing happening in the senate?
How's it the senators sit but make no laws?

    Because the barbarians come today.
    What's the sense of the senators making laws now?
    When the barbarians get here, they'll make the laws.

Why did the emperor come out so early?
Why's he on his throne at the main gate,
wearing his crown?

    Because the barbarians show up today
    and the emperor is waiting to welcome their leader.
    He's all prepared to present an official scroll
    full of titles, important names.

Why have our consuls and praetors appeared
in their scarlet, embroidered togas?
Why their bracelets studded with amethysts,
rings and splendidly sparkling emeralds?
Why do they sport graceful canes
finely worked in silver and gold?

Because the barbarians get here today
and bamboozle like that impresses barbarians.

Where are our public speakers
to make their usual speeches?

    The barbarians come today
    and baloney bores barbarians.

Why this restlessness now, this confusion?
People's faces have turned so serious.
Why's the square emptying?
Why's everyone going home so upset?

    Because it's night and the barbarians haven't come.
    Some border men just in say
    there are no barbarians anymore.

So now? Without the barbarians what will become of us?
Those barbarians were a sort of solution.

                        November 1898

One of Their Gods

When one of them crossed the square
of Selefkia about nightfall —
a tall, strikingly handsome young man,
the radiance of immortality in his eyes,
his groomed black hair perfumed —
passing couples would eye him
asking each other if they knew him,
if he was a Syrian Greek or a visitor.
The more sensitive understood and stepped aside.
Then, as he was lost from sight under the arcades,
between the shadows and the evening lights,
making for that quarter that comes alive only at night
in drink and debauchery,
they would wonder which one of Them
he might be, for what curious indulgence
he had come down to the streets of Selefkia
from those August Heavenly Mansions.

June 1899

Thermopylae

Honour to those who, in their lifetimes,
dedicate themselves to defend their Thermopylae.
They never shirk responsibility,
just and equitable in all they do,
with compassion, with pity.
Generous when wealthy; when in want
still giving in their way,
helpful as possible;
always truthful, above
despising the liar.

And they are worthy of greater honour
when they foresee, and many do,
that an Ephialtes will show up in the end,
that in the long run the Persians will get through.

January 1901

Come Back

Come back frequently and hold me.
Secret sensation come back,
embrace and take me when the flesh reawakes
and this tired body's lust pumps blood again
when fingertips touch, tantalise all over.

Come back. Hold me through the night
as fresh bodies recall, mouths remind . . .

June 1904

I Went

I didn't hesitate, I went;
went into the fluorescent night,
to satisfactions sometimes real
at times icons of inspiration.
I drank deep, as only connoisseurs
of concupiscence drink.

June 1905

He Swears

Some days he swears he'll begin a better life,
but when night comes on with its own notions,
its possibilities and its compromises;
when night creeps up with its peculiar powers
of the body's desires, demands,
he returns lost to the same pernicious pleasures.

December 1905

One Night

The room was vulgar, squalid,
hidden above that questionable tavern.
You could see the narrow, filthy alley
from the window and hear the voices
of workmen happily drinking
and playing cards below.

There, on that commonplace bed,
I possessed love's body, had those sensuous
lips, that red, voluptuous mouth
so that now, as I write, after so many years,
in this my lonely house, I'm drugged with desire again.

July 1907

29

The Tobacco Shop

They stood among others
at the lit window of a tobacco shop.
Their eyes met, shyly — hesitantly
expressed bodily cravings. Then,
some anxious steps along the pavement
until the smile, the nod.

Next, the closed carriage,
sensual body touch,
holding of hands,
touching of lips.

September 1907

Days of 1903

I never found them again — gone so fast . . .
those poetic eyes, that pale face . . .
in the dark street . . .

I never found them again — taken so easily,
then dropped so casually.
Poetic eyes, pale face,
those lips — lost forever.

March 1909

So Much Beauty

I've seen so much beauty
my vision is full with it.

The body's contours. Red lips. Sensual limbs.
Hair chiselled as in Greek sculptures
still lovely even when tousled,
tumbling a little over pale foreheads.
Images of love, as my poems desired them . . .
met in youthful nights, secretly.

October 1911

Rites of Passage

All a schoolboy timidly imagines
now opens to him. Sleepless, he cruises
town, drifts astray. And, rightly,
(for our art) we pleasure in his fresh
urgent blood. His body is overcome
by forbidden pleasures; his limp limbs
abandon themselves youthfully.
So a simple boy deserves admiration.
He passes briefly through the sublime World
of Poetry — the sensitive boy with youth's hot blood.

January 1914

33

Long Ago

I remember . . .
vague now . . . so little left . . .
long ago . . . my adolescence.

Jasmine skin . . .
an August evening . . . August?
I vaguely remember the eyes: blue, I think . . .
Yes. . . Yes indeed; sapphire blue.

March 1914

At The Café Door

Some remark beside me turned
my eyes towards the door.
That adorable body stood there,
created as if by Eros himself
pleasurably modelling the limbs,
shaping the delicate features
with touches of fingertips,
leaving a felt finish
on brow, eyes, mouth.

June? 1915

Nero's Deadline

Nero wasn't upset by the prophesy of the Delphic Oracle:
"Fear the seventy-third year".
Nero, only thirty, had plenty of time to live his comedy.
The reign granted him by the god looks long enough
to find time for fears of the future.

Now, vaguely bored, he will return to Rome,
divinely tired after this trip of nothing but pleasure:
round the gardens, in the theatre, at the games . . .
The cities of Greece at evening . . .
especially the feel of fervent flesh.

That's Nero. In Spain, Galba
secretly musters and drills his troops.
Galba, the old man of seventy-three.

December 1915

One Evening

It wouldn't have lasted anyway.
Experience over the years taught me that.
The finality of Fate shocks when it strikes.
The largesse of that life stopped short.
How pungent the perfumes then,
how lazy the bed we lay on,
what indulgences we allowed ourselves.

An echo of those days of pleasure
came back to me, a spark
of that fire of young love.
I took out a letter once more,
read it several times till the light failed.

Saddened, I moved out onto the balcony
to brush off those thoughts by gazing
again over this city I love,
the movement in the streets, in the shops.

July 1907

Remember, Body

Remember, body, not only those beds
you lay on, how much you were loved there,
but also the blatant desire that shone
in those eyes for you, trembled on those tongues . . .

Now that they have all sunk in the past
it seems you may have given in to those desires.
Remember how it lit those eyes on you,
trembled for you in those voices.
Remember, body.

May 1916

In a Town of Osroini

They brought our friend Remon back
late last night. Wounded in a bar brawl.
Through the wide open window the moon
lit up his beautiful body on the bed.
We're a mixed bunch here: Greeks, Asians.
Remon is one of our own. Last night,
while the moon illuminated his sensual face,
we thought of Plato's Charmidis.

August 1916

Grey

Admiring a half-grey opal
I recalled two lovely grey eyes
of, surely, twenty years ago . . .

We were lovers for a month.
Then he left for work. In Smyrna I think.
Haven't seen him since.

Those grey eyes are aged now . . .
if he's still alive. His fine features also . . .

O Memory, preserve them as they were.
Bring me back all you can, bring back
anything you can, tonight.

February 1917

The Month Of Athyr

I can barely make out
     on this ancient stone
L[O]RD JESUS CHRIST.
     I also make out SO[U]L
IN THE MON[TH] OF ATHYR
LEFKIO[S] FEL[L] A[SL]EEP.
     I decipher his age.
HE LI[V]ED . . . YEARS.
The Kappa Zeta shows
     he died young.
On the corroded bit I spell
HE [WAS] ALEXANDRIAN.
     Then follow three lines
     hopelessly damaged,
     but I make out
OUR TEA[R]S . . . GRIEF
     and again TEARS.
Then W[E] HIS [F]RIENDS GRIEV[E].
It seems that Lefkios
     was dearly loved
and in the month of Athyr
     Lefkios went to sleep.

March 1917

Tomb of Iasis

I, Iasis, lie here. In this great city
I was famous for my good looks.
The intelligent admired me.
Likewise the louts. I revelled in both.

Eventually, overplaying Narcissus and Hermes
drained, destroyed me. Passerby, if you're
Alexandrian you'll not blame me.
You know the pitch and pace of our lifestyle,
its passionate indulgence, delight in decadence.

April 1917

That House

Yesterday, wandering in a peripheral
district, I passed that house
I used to frequent as a young fellow.
Love, with his marvellous strength,
possessed my body there.

And yesterday
as I meandered along the old road,
of a sudden the flagstones, the shops,
the footpath, walls, balconies, windows
were all transformed by the power of love.
Nothing ugly remained.

While I stopped and stared at the door,
stood lingering outside that house,
my very being radiated
all its pent up passion.

July 1917

Since Nine O'Clock

Half-past twelve. Time has passed so quickly
since nine when I lit the lamp and sat down.
I've been sitting here without reading or speaking.
Alone in this house there's nobody to talk to.

Since I lit the lamp at nine
the appearance of my young body
has comforted me, reminding me
of closed, scented rooms,
passions long dead, reckless risks.
It also revived memories of forgotten streets,
public places alive with people now gone,
theatres and coffee tables of long ago.

That vision of my youthful body
also brought sad memories:
separations, family grief,
the sentiments of my own people, feelings
for the dead so poorly appreciated alive.

Half-past twelve. Time passes.
Half-past twelve. The years pass.

November 1917

At Rest in Verse

It was about one o'clock in the morning,
or half-past.

        A corner of a tavern,
behind the wooden partition.
Except for the pair of us the place was empty.
One lamp hardly lit it.
The waiter dozed near the door.

Nobody could see us.
Anyway we were so turned on
we didn't give a damn.

Our scant clothes were already wide open
and divine July was roasting.

Quick baring of bodies,
fleshy feel between half open clothes.
A flash-back to twenty six years ago
has passed but remains at rest
in these verses.

March 1918

On Board Ship

This little pencil sketch
certainly resembles him.

Done quickly out on deck
one magic afternoon
the Ionian Sea spread all around us.

It's a likeness. But I remember him more handsome.
He looked sensitive to the point of sanctity
and that gave luminosity to his expression.
He seems better looking to me
now that my soul conjures him out of Time.

Out of Time. These things from way back then —
the sketch, the ship, the afternoon.

October 1919

Those who Fought for the Achaian League

You who fought and fell were truly brave,
unafraid of an enemy who was winning hands down.
You were blameless if Diaios and Kritolaos were wrong.
When Greeks want to boast they will say :
"They're the kind of men our nation produces".
That's how proudly they'll praise you.

Written by an Achaian in Alexandria
in the seventh year of Ptolemy Lathyros' reign.

February 1922

He Came to Read

He came to read. Two, three
books by historians, poets, propped open.
He barely read ten minutes,
then stopped and dozed off on the divan.
He's totally devoted to books.
At twenty-three he's very attractive;
and this afternoon Eros coursed
through his ideal body, his lips.
The fervour of love in flesh
that seems the apotheosis of beauty —
feeling no shame at the sheer pleasure of it . . .

July ? 1924

AFTERWORD

When I first read the poems of C.P. Cavafy in the 1950s I saw him, and still do today, as a modernist, indeed as a cubist poet. I also realised that he had been so as early as the 1890s but had remained generally unknown in the west until after his death in 1933.

Born in 1863 a singular person in a singular place at the dawn of that singular manifestation we call Western Modernism, Cavafy was one of the first rays of light of that dawn. Alone on the south-eastern fringe of Europe, on the coast of Egypt at Alexandria, Cavafy discovered a modern persona in himself who in turn deliberately created, from his mundane daily life and his mytho-historic view of it, a corpus of poetry that is a cornerstone of modern western literature. His theme was history – ancient empirical, modern personal. As a poet his point of view was elitist. And if there's nothing new in that, it was the way Cavafy personalised his past as a Greek Alexandrian in the present that was new, that was modernist, that was Cubist – a movement that did not begin publicly until 1907 and ended in 1914 with the First World War.

Herbert Reed has written: "Cubism deals principally with forms and when a form is realised it is there to live its own life which is communicated by the subject but recreated in the object. Cubism does not analyse the subject, it is an individual act of perception". The artist/poet is the transitive agent between subject and object. In the early 1890s in the poems 'Footsteps' using Nero, 'Ithaka' using Odysseus, 'The City' using Alexandria, 'The First Step' using Theocritus, 'Expecting the Barbarians' and 'Thermopylae', among others, Cavafy was realising the possibility of a modern, multi-dimensional poetry of the historical and mythical imagination that was simultaneously epiphanic, naturalistically, symbolically, metaphorically, historically and mythically. That is Cubism.

I am not saying that Cavafy deliberately chose a Cubist perspective, any more than Cezanne, Picasso or Braque did. My suggestion is that at an early stage, Cavafy's way of seeing, his perception of his world was not dissimilar to that of mature Cezanne and of Picasso and Braque and that they made their individual art accordingly. Cavafy's epiphany had been to see that the squalid, by-passed, declining, historic Alexandria of his own day was the stage on which to present his perception of Alexandria during the last three centuries BC and the first four centuries AD (with a cast familiar to the educated world) in demotic, or spoken, Greek with some purist, or refined, and Byzantine Greek inset when it served his purpose – the history of his language. He saw how to record in poems his personal (actual and imagined) life in historic Alexandria for like-minded other persons, including his own "other person".

Ten years later, between 1903 and 1907 James Joyce, knowing nothing of Cavafy, saw this possibility for prose while writing certain stories of 'Dubliners' and expanded it in his 'Ulysses'. In 1906-7 Picasso painted his unfinished Les Demoiselles d'Avignon while contemporaneously Schoenberg played polytonal music, Brancusi displaced his sculpturable space and Einstein explained space-time in his Cubist special theory of Relativity – not to mention Freud and Jung. But all that was at the centre of empire where everybody knew about everybody else. By 1906-7, out on the fringe of empire, standing cubistically alone at his own angle to the universe in his own cultural loneliness, Cavafy had already done it for poetry as a maturely objective, dispassionate, properly ambiguous and elitist poet – and apparently without benefit of outside influence.

Cavafy became his own place, period, paraphernalia, persona and poem simultaneously, and his youthful Eros matured into *agape,* or brotherly love.

—*Desmond O'Grady. Kinsale, 1998*